Flavoured Oils and Vinegars

Flavoured Oils and Vinegars

Love Food ® is an imprint of Parragon Books Ltd

Parragon
Queen Street House
4 Queen Street
Bath BA1 1HE, UK

Copyright © Parragon Books Ltd 2007

Love Food ® and the accompanying heart device is a trademark of Parragon Books Ltd

ISBN 978-1-4075-1745-2

Printed in China

Text by Ann Kleinberg
Edited by Lorraine Turner
Produced by the Buenavista Studio s.l.
Photography by Günter Beer
Home Economy by Stevan Paul
Design by Cammaert & Eberhardt

Notes for the reader

This book uses metric and imperial measurements. Follow the same units of measurement
throughout; do not mix metric and imperial. All spoon measurements are level: teaspoons
are assumed to be 5 ml, and tablespoons are assumed to be 15 ml. Unless otherwise stated,
milk is assumed to be full-fat, eggs and vegetables such as potatoes are medium, and
pepper is freshly ground black pepper. Recipes using raw or very lightly cooked eggs should
not be served to children, the elderly, pregnant women, convalescents and anyone suffering
from an illness. The times given are approximate only.

Contents

Introduction

Oils and vinegars have appeared on our tables for thousands of years. Evidence has been found in ancient Greek and Egyptian writings, biblical texts and archaeological finds to suggest that early civilizations appreciated the taste and versatility of these delicious ingredients. How wonderful that something so ancient and venerated is still an integral part of our cuisine today.

In addition to its importance as a cooking medium, oil serves as a preservative (think sun-dried tomatoes, sardines and olives) and as the basis for most dressings. One might say that oil is the soul of a salad, providing a foundation for all the other ingredients. Is there anything more perfect than a lovely green salad dressed with a fine olive oil and a sprinkle of fresh lemon juice?

Vinegar came to us by accident, and what a happy accident it was! A vat of grape juice that was intended for wine was probably left open or fermented too long, and the result, known in French as 'vinaigre' or 'sour wine', was the mother of what has now become a vast vinegar industry.

Suddenly the world is taking notice of oils and vinegars – and it is about time! You can enjoy them just as they are, but why not be a bit experimental? Infused with herbs, spices, nuts or fruit, oils and vinegars take on a whole new life, adding a wonderful flavour dimension. The essence of the flavour soaks into the dish and upgrades it to something a little more special.

The versatility of flavoured oils and vinegars never ceases to amaze, and this book will provide the basis for wonderful recipes to inspire and delight. The process is so simple: follow the guidelines, use caution and have fun. Use the recipes presented here or let your imagination run wild and flavour with your own combinations.

Introduction to Oils

Edible oil has a rich history shared by many cultures over many centuries. It is used as a cooking medium, a preservative, a medicine and, best of all, food. The Chinese and Japanese developed methods to extract oil from soya plants; Mediterranean people use olives; Mexicans and North Americans are fond of peanuts and sunflower seeds; and in Africa, palms and coconuts provide the basis for oil. Other sources of oil are cotton, safflower seeds, watermelon seeds, grape seeds, rapeseed, corn, nuts, avocados and, of course, animals.

Thanks to the popularity of the Mediterranean diet, olive oil has captured the world's attention with its health-inducing benefits. Other beneficial oils, such as rapeseed, are almost flavourless and present the perfect backdrop for flavourful additions.

There are just a few guidelines to follow before getting started. The most important to remember is this: oil improperly stored can encourage the growth of bacteria. When herbs or vegetables with a high water content (like garlic) are mixed with oil and stored in a non-refrigerated place, an oxygen-free environment is created that can lead to botulism. Careful preparation and refrigerated storage will prevent problems.

The following points are important to remember:

1. Invest in some good glass jars and sterilize them (pour boiling water over them and leave them to stand for 10 minutes). Do not use cheap jars – the metal ring may rust and the rubber seals may disintegrate.
2. Rapeseed oil is a perfect base for most flavourings because it does not have a distinctive flavour. Olive oil is great for the heartier herbs that can handle its strong flavour.
3. Bruising or crumbling herbs before adding them to the oil releases their flavour.
4. Heating the oil will help infuse the flavour of the added ingredients.
5. Make small amounts and always store flavoured oils in the refrigerator.
6. Remove from the refrigerator and bring to room temperature before using.

Basil Oil

The concept of flavoured oils must have been designed with basil in mind. There are so many recipes for basil and oil - why not mix them and be ahead of the game?

25g/1 oz fresh basil leaves

2 garlic cloves, halved

250 ml/9 fl oz olive oil

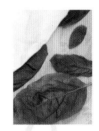

Wash the basil leaves and dry them well. Prepare a bowl of iced water.

Bring a saucepan of water to the boil, add the basil leaves and blanch for 5 seconds. Scoop out the leaves and plunge immediately into the iced water to stop the cooking process. Drain out all the water and squeeze the leaves to get rid of as much of the water as possible. Dry them between layers of kitchen paper. Chop roughly and place in a clean jar. Add the garlic.

Gently heat the oil over a low heat until warmed and fragrant - about 5 minutes. Make sure it does not boil or burn. Remove from the heat and pour the oil into a clean jar over the basil leaves. Leave to cool, cover and store in the refrigerator. Strain out the basil within a week.

Note: the olive oil has a very dominant flavour. If you prefer a stronger basil flavour, use rapeseed oil instead.

Mint Oil

You will look for excuses to use this wonderful oil - it is so refreshing and, well, minty!

25 g/1 oz mint leaves

250 ml/9 fl oz rapeseed oil

Wash and dry the mint leaves. Prepare a bowl of iced water.

Bring a saucepan of water to the boil, add the mint leaves, making sure that they are all submerged, and blanch for 5 seconds. Scoop out the leaves using a slotted spoon and plunge immediately into the iced water. Drain, squeezing out all the water from the leaves. Dry the leaves between layers of kitchen paper.

Roughly chop the leaves and add to a blender or food processor. Pour in some of the oil and process. Add more oil, continuing to process until all the oil is added. Scrape the blender or processor with a rubber spatula, and process again, making sure that all the leaves are finely minced and well combined with the oil.

Strain through muslin and then pour into a clean jar. Refrigerate until ready to use. Bring to room temperature before use.

Tomato, Mozzarella and Basil Kebabs

12 cherry or plum tomatoes

12 fresh basil leaves, or more

12 baby mozzarella balls

basil oil

freshly ground black pepper

Makes 12 skewers

Making this tasty dish is easy. Just put together the ingredients (and add any of your own), skewer them and serve to your delighted guests.

Cut the tomatoes in half crossways. Wash and dry the basil leaves.

Thread each skewer with a tomato half, a basil leaf, and a baby mozzarella ball. Add another tomato half to the end.

Arrange the skewers on a serving platter, drizzle them with the basil oil, sprinkle with a little black pepper and serve.

Bruschetta with Tomato, Red Onion and Basil Salsa

1 large baguette or focaccia loaf

2 tbsp **basil oil**

Basil salsa

10 plum tomatoes

2 red onions

10 g/¹⁄₄ oz basil leaves (green or purple)

juice of 2 lemons

salt and freshly ground black pepper

Serves 6

This is a wonderful idea for a Mediterranean-style lunch or snack. Serve it alongside a simple salad with a chilled bottle of white wine.

Preheat the oven to 230ºC/450ºF/Gas Mark 8.

Slice open the baguette. Place on a baking sheet, brush with some of the basil oil, place in the oven and toast until golden.

To make the salsa, blanch the tomatoes in boiling water for about 5 seconds to allow for the easy removal of the skin. Plunge the tomatoes into some iced water. Peel, slice in half, deseed and dice. Chop the red onions and basil leaves.

Combine the tomatoes, onions and basil with the lemon juice and the remaining basil oil. Season with salt and pepper to taste. Spoon the salsa over each slice of toasted bread and serve.

Yogurt Soup with Pomegranates and Mint Oil

900 ml/1 ½ pints natural yogurt

3 whole cucumbers, peeled and diced

4 garlic cloves, minced

3 tbsp finely chopped fresh dill, plus extra to garnish

3 tbsp finely chopped fresh mint leaves

juice of ½ lemon

salt

white pepper

20 g/¾ oz pomegranate seeds

mint oil

mint oil ice cubes

Serves 4

This soup is so easy to make, so refreshing to drink and tastes absolutely delicious.

In a large mixing bowl, combine the yogurt, cucumbers, garlic, dill, mint leaves and lemon juice. Season with salt and pepper to taste. Chill for several hours.

Pour the yogurt soup into soup bowls, garnish with the pomegranate seeds, chopped dill and a drizzle of the mint oil. If you have them to hand, add a few mint oil ice cubes.

Note: prepare the mint oil ice cubes in advance by pouring the mint oil into ice cube trays. Freeze and use whenever desired.

Garlic, Chilli and Oregano Oil

Put some of this deliciously spicy oil on a plate, serve with warm, crusty bread, some cheese and olives, and you will have a Mediterranean feast!

5 garlic cloves

2 tbsp red hot chilli

1 tsp dried oregano

250 ml/9 fl oz rapeseed oil

Preheat the oven to 150°C/300°F/Gas Mark 2.

Cut the garlic cloves in half lengthways. Using gloves, remove the seeds from the chilli and chop the flesh into small pieces equalling 2 tablespoons.

Combine the garlic, chilli and oregano with the oil in an ovenproof glass dish. Place in the centre of the oven and heat for 1½-2 hours. The temperature of the oil should reach 120°C/250°F if you are using a digital thermometer.

Remove from the oven, leave to cool and then strain through muslin into a clean jar. Store covered in the refrigerator. You can also leave the garlic and chilli pieces in the oil and strain before using.

Parsley and Coriander Oil

This oil is so fresh-tasting and green! It can be sprinkled on soup or used as a dressing for salads. Feel free to change the ratio of leaves if you prefer one herb over the other.

10 g/¼ oz fresh parsley leaves

10 g/¼ oz fresh coriander leaves

250 ml/9 fl oz rapeseed oil

Wash and drain the leaves. Prepare a pot of water, bring to the boil and sub-merge the leaves. Blanch for 5 seconds. Drain the leaves and dry well.

Heat the oil in a saucepan, bring almost to the boil and allow to simmer for 1-2 minutes.

Combine the warmed oil and leaves in a blender bowl or food processor. Process until well combined.

Pour through muslin and strain into a clean jar. Cover and refrigerate.

Roasted Antipasti with Garlic, Chilli and Oregano Oil

1 medium sweet potato, peeled and cut into chunks

2 fennel bulbs, quartered

2 leeks, white parts only, cut diagonally into 5-cm/2-inch pieces

1 head garlic, cut in half horizontally

10 shallots, peeled

125 ml/4 fl oz **garlic, chilli and oregano oil**

2 tbsp coarse salt

Serves 6

These vegetables are only a suggestion. Choose any seasonal vegetables, sprinkle with the wonderfully aromatic garlic, chilli and oregano oil, and roast away!

Preheat the oven to 230°C/450°F/Gas Mark 8.

Arrange all the vegetables on a baking tray or sheet. Brush with the garlic, chilli and oregano oil and sprinkle with salt. Place in the oven and roast for 20 to 25 minutes. Some of the vegetables may soften sooner than others, so keep an eye on them and remove those first.

Remove the tray from the oven, brush the vegetables with a little more of the flavoured oil, and serve.

Focaccia with Tomato, Mozzarella and Red Onion

Focaccia

1 tsp easy-blend dried yeast

250 ml/9 fl oz warm water

1 tbsp sugar

350 g/12 oz plain flour, plus extra for dusting

1 tsp salt

4 tbsp olive oil

Topping

garlic, chilli and oregano oil

4 plum tomatoes, thinly sliced

1 red onion, thinly sliced

$1/2$ tsp coarse salt

200 g/7 oz mozzarella, sliced

5 g/$1/8$ oz fresh basil leaves, torn

Makes 1 large loaf

Any combination of ingredients can be used for the toppings, but these work beautifully with the delicious garlic, chilli and oregano oil.

In a large mixing bowl, combine the yeast, half of the warm water, the sugar and 1 tablespoon of the flour. Leave to stand for about 10 minutes until it bubbles and becomes foamy.

Add the remaining water and flour and the salt. Using a dough hook, mix all the ingredients together. Gradually pour in the oil and continue to mix until a ball is formed. Cover the bowl with clingfilm, set it in a warm place and leave the dough to rise for 1 hour. It should double in size.

Preheat the oven to 230-240°C/450-475°F/Gas Mark 8-9. Grease a baking sheet and sprinkle a little flour on it. Punch down the ball of dough and, using oiled hands, spread it out over the entire baking sheet. Let it rise for 10 minutes.

Using your fingertips or the back of a spoon, punch dimples into the dough.

Brush some of the garlic, chilli and oregano oil on to the dough, and cover it with slices of tomato and onion. Sprinkle with the coarse salt and pour on a little more of the flavoured oil. Bake for 15 minutes.

Remove from the oven, add the slices of mozzarella, and return it to the oven for another 5 minutes or until the cheese melts.

Remove the focaccia from the oven, sprinkle with torn basil leaves, cut into squares and serve.

Tuna Ceviche with Parsley and Coriander Oil

200 g/7 oz red tuna fillet
(about 1 serving)

1 medium red onion, diced

1 red pepper, diced

4 tbsp lemon juice

1 lemon, grated zest only

3 tbsp orange juice

5 tbsp **parsley and coriander oil**

¼ tsp chopped ginger

½ tsp chopped chilli

2 tbsp balsamic vinegar

salt and freshly ground black pepper

flat-leaf parsley leaves, to garnish

crackers, to serve

Serves 2

Ceviche is not difficult to make, as this recipe will demonstrate, and the result will prove that some things are best when kept simple!

Chop the tuna into very small pieces. Combine with the remaining ingredients, mix well, cover and chill for at least 1 hour in the refrigerator before serving.

Serve with crackers and add a few parsley leaves, to garnish.

Roasted Tomato Oil

This versatile oil tastes divine on almost anything - try it on pizza, pasta or focaccia for a tasty treat.

4-6 plum tomatoes

250 ml/9 fl oz rapeseed oil

Preheat the oven to 200°C/400°F/Gas Mark 6.

Thinly slice the tomatoes and place them on a lightly greased baking sheet. Place in the oven and roast until they start to char. Remove from the oven and leave to cool.

Heat the oil in a saucepan. Bring almost to the boil and allow to simmer for 1-2 minutes.

Combine the tomatoes with the warmed oil, and process in a blender or food processor. Process until the tomatoes are well incorporated into the oil. Strain through muslin and pour into a clean jar. Refrigerate.

Lemon Pepper Oil

Pasta, chicken and fish complement the flavours of this oil particularly well, but it is a good staple to keep in the kitchen because it works well with almost anything.

zest of 1 lemon

1 whole lemon

2 tsp multi-coloured peppercorns

250 ml/9 fl oz olive oil

Prepare a double boiler. Bring the water in the bottom pan to the boil, lower the heat and simmer.

Cut the lemon zest into thin strips, making sure you omit the white pith. Thinly slice the other lemon. Crush the peppercorns using a mortar and pestle. Put the strips of lemon zest, lemon slices, peppercorns and olive oil in the top of the double boiler.

Cook over simmering water for 1 hour. The oil should reach a temperature of 120°C/250°F, tested with a digital or sugar thermometer. Make sure you don't let the oil burn.

Remove from the heat, leave to cool and then strain through muslin into a clean jar. Cover and store in the refrigerator. You can also leave the lemon strips and pepper in the jar and refrigerate, and then strain before using.

Quinoa Salad with Sun-dried Tomatoes, Black Olives and Feta

Salad

235 g/8 ½ oz quinoa

500 ml/18 fl oz water

10 sun-dried tomatoes (in oil, drained)

50 g/1 ¾ oz feta cheese, crumbled

2 spring onions, white parts, chopped

20 g/ ¾ oz mixed fresh herbs (basil, parsley, coriander), chopped

50 g/1 ¾ oz stoned black olives, chopped

Dressing

5 tbsp **roasted tomato oil**

3 tbsp fresh lemon juice

1 garlic clove, crushed

salt and freshly ground black pepper

Serves 4

This salad is perfect as a main course or as a side dish for chicken or fish. It is delicious, colourful and really good for you!

Spread the quinoa on a dish and pick out any pieces of grit. Rinse the grains thoroughly in a fine-mesh sieve and drain.

In a medium saucepan, bring the water to the boil over a high heat, stir in the quinoa and return to the boil. Lower the heat, cover, and simmer for about 15 minutes or until all the liquid has been absorbed. Remove from the heat, fluff up the quinoa with a fork and transfer to a bowl. Leave to cool a little.

Add the remaining ingredients to the bowl and mix with the quinoa.

Whisk the dressing ingredients together, pour over the quinoa, toss and serve.

Fettuccine with Lemon Pepper Seafood

5 tbsp **lemon pepper oil**, plus extra for serving

6 garlic cloves, crushed

675 g/1½ lb mixed seafood (prawns, squid, mussels)

dash of vodka

125 ml/4 fl oz white wine

1 sprig tarragon, leaves only

dash of salt

450 g/1 lb fettuccine

chopped flat-leaf parsley, to garnish

Serves 4

This is a great dinner-party dish because it can be prepared in minutes, but your guests will never know from the delicious taste!

Heat a wok or deep frying pan and add the lemon pepper oil. When the oil is hot, add the garlic and seafood. Stir for 1 minute. Add a dash of vodka, the white wine, tarragon leaves and salt. Keep stirring until the seafood is cooked through.

Prepare the fettuccine according to the directions on the packet. When the fettuccine is cooked, drain and add to the seafood mixture. Toss well and serve immediately on warmed plates. Drizzle more lemon pepper oil on top to serve and garnish with the chopped parsley.

Rosemary, Lemon and Thyme Oil

You may want to make this just for the glorious aroma that permeates the house as the oil is heating.

5 sprigs rosemary
(each about 13 cm/5 inches long)

10 to 15 sprigs thyme
(each about 13 cm/5 inches long)

zest of 2 lemons

250 ml/9 fl oz rapeseed oil

Preheat the oven to 150°C/300°F/Gas Mark 2.

Remove the leaves from the rosemary and thyme sprigs. Cut the lemon zest into strips.

Pour the oil into an ovenproof glass dish and add the leaves and lemon zest strips. Place the dish in the centre of the oven and heat for 1 ½-2 hours.

If you have a digital thermometer, test the oil. It should reach a temperature of 120°C/250°F before you remove it from the oven. Leave to cool for at least 30 minutes.

Store the oil in the refrigerator as it is, or strain through muslin and refrigerate.

Lemon Grass and Lime Oil

Lemon grass is a treasured ingredient in South-east Asian cuisine and tastes even better when paired with lime.

10 stalks lemon grass

zest of 1 lime

$\frac{1}{2}$ lime

250 ml/9 fl oz rapeseed oil

Preheat the oven to 150°C/300°F/Gas Mark 2.

Wash and dry the fresh lemon grass stalks (using the bottom part). Bruise them by crushing or gently pounding to release the flavour. Cut into 7.5-cm/3-inch pieces.

Cut the zest of 1 lime into thin strips, omitting the white pith. Slice the half-lime into thin slices.

Put the lemon grass stalks, lime zest and lime slices in an ovenproof glass dish. Pour in the oil and make sure it covers everything, then transfer to the centre of the oven.

Heat for at least an hour or until the temperature of the oil reaches 120°C/ 250°F. Use a digital thermometer to test.

Remove from the oven, leave to cool and pour into a clean container. Store the oil in the refrigerator as it is, or strain through muslin and refrigerate.

Grilled Lamb Chops in Rosemary, Lemon and Thyme Oil

5 tbsp white wine

5 tbsp **rosemary, lemon and thyme oil**

1 garlic clove, crushed

1/2 tsp chopped rosemary leaves

1/2 tsp chopped thyme leaves

4 portions lamb chops

salt and freshly ground black pepper

To garnish

1 sprig rosemary

zest of 1 lemon, cut into thin strips

Serves 4

This dish looks as impressive as it tastes, and the addition of the oil makes it something very special.

Make the marinade by whisking together the wine, flavoured oil, garlic, and rosemary and thyme leaves. Pour over the lamb chops, making sure each piece gets covered, cover the dish with clingfilm, and refrigerate for up to 3 hours.

Remove the chops from the refrigerator and leave them to sit at room temperature for about 30 minutes before grilling.

Heat the grill to medium-high. Sprinkle salt and pepper over the lamb chops and grill on both sides until cooked to your taste.

Garnish with a rosemary sprig and strips of lemon zest.

Roasted Chicken with Rosemary, Lemon and Thyme Oil Rub

4 tbsp **rosemary, lemon and thyme oil**

1 roasting chicken
(2.25-2.7 kg/5-6 lbs)

1 large lemon, chopped

1 sprig rosemary

3 garlic cloves

250 g/9 oz coarse salt

Serves 4-6

You might want to make this just for the wonderful aroma that will fill your kitchen when it is roasting!

Brush the rosemary, lemon and thyme oil all over the chicken, cover and then marinate for several hours or overnight.

Preheat the oven to 200°C/400°F/Gas Mark 6. Fill the cavity of the chicken with the chopped lemon pieces, rosemary sprig and garlic cloves. Place the chicken in a roasting tin, surround it with the coarse salt and then roast for 45 minutes to 1 hour. Check that the chicken is cooked by piercing the thickest part of the leg with a sharp knife or skewer and making sure that the juices run clear.

Remove from the oven, cut the chicken into quarters and serve.

Sizzling Lemon Grass Beef with Asparagus and Red Pepper

15 spears asparagus

2 tbsp **lemon grass and lime oil**

200 g/7 oz beansprouts

1 red pepper, thinly sliced

1 tbsp chopped garlic

450 g/1 lb fillet steak, thinly sliced

5 tbsp dry white wine

salt and freshly ground black pepper

zest of 1 lime, cut into thin strips

Serves 4

The combination of flavours and colours in this dish makes for a taste sensation - try adding different vegetables if these are not to your liking.

Clean the asparagus by scraping away any woody parts and trimming off the cut ends, if necessary. Slice each spear diagonally into thirds. Bring a saucepan of water to the boil and quickly blanch the asparagus. Plunge into iced water.

Heat a wok over a high heat and add the lemon grass and lime oil. Add the beansprouts, red pepper, garlic and beef and stir-fry for 1 minute. Add the wine and asparagus, and salt and pepper, and stir-fry until the beef is done. Add the lime zest, stir for another minute and remove from the heat. Place on a serving platter or plates and serve immediately.

Steamed Sea Bass with Lemon Grass and Lime Oil

675-900 g/1^1/$_2$-2 lb whole sea bass, cut open along one side

1 stalk lemon grass (bottom 15 cm/ 6 inches only), thinly sliced

2 garlic cloves, thinly sliced

3 lime slices

salt and freshly ground black pepper

3 tbsp **lemon grass and lime oil**

To garnish

sliced tomatoes

sliced red and green peppers

Serves 1

Serve this fish with cooked new potatoes on the side, and drizzle the potatoes with a little lemon grass and lime oil for something extra special.

Preheat the oven to 220°C/425°F/Gas Mark 7.

   Open up the fish and place the lemon grass, garlic and lime slices inside. Sprinkle with salt and pepper, and a little of the lemon grass and lime oil. Close and make 3 diagonal slits through the skin along the length of the fish on both sides. Brush the outside with the oil and sprinkle on more salt and pepper.

   Lay out a piece of aluminium foil large enough to wrap around the fish. On top of the foil, place a large sheet of baking paper and place the fish on it. Make an envelope out of the baking paper, then fold up the aluminium foil around it (doing so will ensure that the fish is steamed). Place on a baking sheet and put in the oven. Bake for 20 minutes.

   Remove from the oven, take the fish out of its baking envelope and place on a serving platter. For a colourful garnish, serve with slices of tomato and red and green pepper placed on top of the fish.

Walnut Oil

This may be one of the most sumptuous oils. In shops it is very expensive, so make your own and enjoy it on salads, breads and fruit.

160 g/2¼ oz walnuts

250 ml/9 fl oz rapeseed oil

Break up the walnuts and dry roast in a frying pan over a medium heat for about 2 minutes or until they start to give off a fragrant aroma.

Using a microwave-proof container, heat the oil in a microwave on medium-high for 1-2 minutes.

Combine 4 tablespoons of the heated oil with the walnuts, and process in a blender or food processor until the walnuts are finely chopped. Combine with the remaining oil, pour into a clean jar and cover. You may leave the oil out for a day so that it absorbs the nutty flavour, then place it in the refrigerator.

Before using, remove the oil from the refrigerator, bring it to room temperature and strain through muslin. Return to the bottle and use. You can use any remaining chopped nuts as part of the dish you are making.

Orange Spice Oil

Prepare yourself for the most wonderful aroma when this oil is cooking. Try it on sweet breads, rice, fish - the possibilities are endless!

grated peel of 1 orange

20 whole cloves

2 whole bay leaves

1 tsp cinnamon

$1/2$ tsp whole black peppercorns

$1/4$ tsp ground nutmeg

2 tbsp orange juice

250 ml/9 fl oz rapeseed oil

Preheat the oven to 150°C/300°F/Gas Mark 2.

Using a mortar and pestle, pound together the grated orange peel, cloves, bay leaves, cinnamon, peppercorns and nutmeg. Add the orange juice. Mix until it forms a paste.

Transfer the paste to an ovenproof dish and add the rapeseed oil. Place the dish in the centre of the oven and cook for about 1 hour or until the oil reaches 120°C/250°F. Use a digital thermometer to test.

Remove from the oven, allow to cool and strain out the flavourings using muslin or a fine-mesh sieve. Pour the strained oil into a clean jar, cover and refrigerate.

Endive Salad with Roquefort, Figs and Walnut Oil

6 medium endives

200 g/7 oz Roquefort cheese, crumbled

2 fresh (or dried) figs, chopped

60 g/2¼ oz walnuts, chopped

125 ml/4 fl oz **walnut oil**

4 tbsp **fig and spice vinegar**

Serves 6

To make this dish truly special, you will need the addition of the fig and spice vinegar, the recipe for which can be found on page 88. Alternatively, you can use ordinary balsamic vinegar.

Cut off the cores of the endives and separate the leaves. Put the leaves in a bowl and add the cheese, figs and walnut pieces.

Combine the walnut oil with the fig and spice vinegar and whisk well. Pour over the salad ingredients and toss gently.

Divide the salad among 6 plates and serve.

Banana Walnut Bread

250 ml/9 fl oz **walnut oil**

200 g/7 oz sugar

2 eggs

3 very ripe bananas, mashed

280 g/10 oz plain flour

1 tsp bicarbonate of soda

1 tsp baking powder

$\frac{1}{2}$ tsp salt

3 tbsp milk

2 tbsp natural yogurt

$\frac{1}{2}$ tsp vanilla extract

60 g/2$\frac{1}{4}$ oz walnuts, crushed

Makes 1 loaf

Banana bread is loved by children and adults alike, and the addition of the walnut oil makes for a superior taste.

Preheat the oven to 175°C/350°F/Gas Mark 4.

Grease a 30-cm/12-inch loaf tin. In an electric mixer, beat the oil and sugar. Beat in the eggs and mashed bananas.

Combine the dry ingredients, then add to the banana mixture. Add the milk, yogurt and vanilla; beat until blended. Stir in the crushed walnuts and pour the batter into the greased pan.

Bake for 50 minutes to 1 hour or until a skewer inserted into the middle comes out clean.

Orange Spice Muffins

2 large eggs

125 g/4^1/$_2$ oz sugar

1 tsp vanilla extract

^{1}/$_2$ tsp grated lemon zest

pinch of salt

140 g/5 oz plain flour, plus extra for dusting

125 ml/4 fl oz **orange spice oil**

icing sugar, for dusting

strips of orange zest, to decorate

Makes 12

These lovely muffins make a perfect treat for breakfast, brunch or an afternoon snack.

Preheat the oven to 190°C/375°F/Gas Mark 5.

Using an electric mixer, beat the eggs and sugar together. Beat in the vanilla, grated lemon zest and salt. Add the flour and mix well. Slowly add in a stream of the orange spice oil and beat until just blended.

Grease and flour a muffin tin. Spoon the mixture into each indentation, filling it about three-quarters full. Place on the middle rack of the oven and bake for about 30 minutes or until a skewer inserted into the middle comes out clean. Remove from the oven, cool and drop out of the pan. Dust the muffins with icing sugar and add the orange zest to decorate.

Introduction to Vinegars

Our ancestors were very wise about vinegar. The ancient Babylonians used it as a preservative, the Romans drank it, Helen of Troy bathed in it and Cleopatra dissolved a pearl in it to prove that she could consume a fortune in a single meal. It is mentioned numerous times in the Bible, and Hippocrates recommended its therapeutic properties.

As with oils, there are many types of vinegars: balsamic (produced from selected grapes and fermented for a long time), red and white wine vinegar, rice vinegar and cider vinegar. There are also speciality vinegars like raspberry, sherry and champagne vinegar.

Good vinegar can be utilized in so many ways. It is used to prepare and preserve food. It also has health-giving properties: a tablespoon a day of cider vinegar is said to be most beneficial. Even its hygienic properties are well-known; your grandmother was right when she told you that there is nothing like a spray of vinegar for cleaning.

Best of all, vinegar plays an important role in dressings, sauces and mustards. It adds just the right kick to a barbecue sauce; it brings tanginess to a vinaigrette; it sweetens a wine reduction sauce. Infusing vinegar with other flavours is a great way to add yet another layer of aroma and flavour.

Since vinegar is high in acid, it does not allow botulism bacteria to flourish. Flavoured vinegars can be stored in a cool, dark place at first. To prevent mould, make sure that the additions are totally submerged. It is a good idea to store vinegar in the refrigerator after a week or two.

The following points are important to remember:

- Use non-reactive containers (glass, enamel or stainless steel) that have been thoroughly cleaned, but not by metal scouring pads.
- Use good-quality vinegar, fresh herbs that have been washed and dried and spices that are not stale.
- Heating the vinegar and bruising the herbs will help speed the infusion process.
- Strain out solids when the vinegar has reached the flavour that you desire.
- Do not store for extended periods of time.

Dill and Peppercorn Vinegar

The classic combination of dill and peppercorns makes for a very tasty vinegar dressing.

6 sprigs fresh dill

250 ml/9fl oz cider vinegar

1 tsp whole black peppercorns

Wash and dry the dill.

In a saucepan over a medium heat, bring the vinegar to the boil. Lower the heat and simmer for 2 minutes. Add the dill and peppercorns, turn off the heat and leave to sit for several minutes until cooled.

Pour into a clean jar, seal and keep in a dark place until ready to use or refrigerate.

Note: a few pieces of chopped fresh mint can also be added to the vinegar as an interesting additional flavour.

Garlic, Chilli and Red Wine Vinegar

If ever a vinegar came with a kick, this is it!

4 garlic cloves

1-cm/½-inch piece red hot chilli

250 ml/9 fl oz red wine vinegar

Peel the garlic and slice lengthways into quarters. Wearing gloves to prevent direct contact with the chilli, chop and deseed. Put the garlic slices and chilli pieces into a clean jar.

Heat the vinegar in a small saucepan over a medium heat until it starts to bubble around the edges. Remove from the heat and pour the vinegar into the jar with the garlic and chilli. Let it cool, then cover and store. The vinegar can be left in a dark place or refrigerated.

Dill and Peppercorn Vinegar

Cucumber Salad

4-6 cucumbers

$^{1}/_{2}$ red onion, thinly sliced into half rings

10 g/$^{1}/_{4}$ oz dill, finely chopped

125 ml/4 fl oz **dill and peppercorn vinegar**

2 tbsp sugar

salt and white pepper

Serves 4-6

This refreshing salad is great for a picnic on a summer's day. Try serving it with cold poached salmon.

Wash and dry the cucumbers and score them lengthways with a fork. (You can also use a vegetable peeler and leave thin strips of peel on.) Slice into very thin slices. Combine with the onions and dill.

Whisk together the vinegar, sugar, and salt and pepper to taste. Pour over the cucumber mixture, toss well and cover. Refrigerate and allow to marinate for several hours.

Garlic and Chilli Barbecue Marinade

one 350-g/12-oz jar preserved apricots

5 tbsp **garlic, chilli and red wine vinegar**

4 tbsp brown sugar

2 garlic cloves, crushed

2 tbsp Dijon mustard

1 tsp grated fresh ginger

Makes about 500 ml/18 fl oz

This barbecue marinade is perfect on almost anything. Try it on ribs, chops or chicken and transform your barbecue food!

Combine all the marinade ingredients in a blender and process until smooth. Cover and refrigerate.

Note: if using the marinade for chicken pieces or spare ribs, it is best to marinate them overnight and then head straight to the barbecue!

Garlic, Chilli and Red Wine Vinegar

Spicy Icy Gazpacho

½ onion, roughly chopped

2 garlic cloves, crushed

3 tbsp olive oil

4 tbsp **garlic, chilli and red wine vinegar**

900 g/2 lb tomatoes

1 large cucumber, peeled and chopped

1 green pepper, roughly chopped

½ stalk celery, sliced

5 g/⅛ oz fresh coriander leaves

4 tbsp tomato purée

125 ml/4 fl oz tomato juice, for thinning (optional)

salt and freshly ground black pepper

parsley and coriander oil ice cubes (optional)

Serves 6-8

A twist on the Spanish classic, the addition of the garlic, chilli and red wine vinegar makes this even better than the original!

Combine all the ingredients, except the tomato juice and salt and pepper, in a food processor and process until a chunky purée forms. Add tomato juice if a thinner consistency is desired. Season with salt and pepper to taste.

Pour into a container, cover and refrigerate for several hours. Remove from the refrigerator immediately before serving.

Note: if you have parsley and coriander oil (see page 21) to hand, freeze some in ice-cube trays and float three in each bowl of gazpacho.

Caraway and Cider Vinegar

A drizzle of this flavourful vinegar goes a long way. It is especially good for all kinds of fresh and cooked cabbage dishes.

1 tbsp caraway seeds

250 ml/9 fl oz cider vinegar

In a dry frying pan, heat the caraway seeds for 1–2 minutes.

In a saucepan over a medium heat, heat the vinegar until it starts to bubble around the edges of the pan.

Add the toasted caraway seeds to the vinegar, pour into a clean jar, cover and store in a dark place.

Mango, Tarragon and Champagne Vinegar

Champagne is definitely not just for drinking on special occasions. Try this recipe using champagne vinegar and make your own special occasion!

4-5 sprigs tarragon

250 ml/9 fl oz champagne vinegar

90 g/3¼ oz mango, diced

4 tbsp orange juice

4 tbsp sugar

¼ tsp vanilla

dash of salt

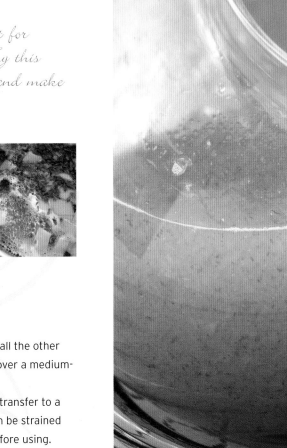

Chop the tarragon leaves and combine with all the other ingredients in a saucepan. Bring to the boil over a medium-high heat and simmer for 1-2 minutes.

Remove from the heat, leave to cool and transfer to a blender. Purée until smooth. The vinegar can be strained and stored, or stored as it is and strained before using. Keep covered in a clean jar in a dark place or refrigerate.

Beetroot and Caraway Borscht

3 tbsp olive oil

1 tbsp caraway seeds

2 medium onions, chopped

3 garlic cloves, crushed

1 potato, peeled and diced

1.4 litres/2½ pints vegetable stock

4 tbsp **caraway and cider vinegar**

900 g/ 2 lb cooked beetroot, diced

salt and freshly ground black pepper

1 tbsp lemon juice

30 g/1¼ oz parsley and coriander, chopped, plus extra to garnish

soured cream, to serve

Serves 4

The colour of this soup is lovely and the taste is exquisite!

Heat a large saucepan over a medium-high heat, add the olive oil and sauté the caraway seeds for 1 minute. Add the onions and stir until they become translucent. Add the garlic and stir in.

Add the potato to the pan, sauté for a few minutes, then add the stock and vinegar. Bring to the boil over a high heat. Lower the heat and simmer for about 8 minutes. Add the cooked beetroot, and salt and pepper, and bring to the boil again. Lower the heat, partly cover the pot, and simmer for 30 to 45 minutes or until the potatoes are cooked through.

Add the lemon juice and herbs and cook for 5 more minutes. Taste and adjust the seasonings.

When the soup cools a little, remove one-third of it to a blender or food processor and process until puréed. Return to the pan, mix, reheat and serve.

Serve the soup with a dollop of soured cream and additional chopped herbs.

Caraway and Cider Vinegar

Braised Red Cabbage and Apples

1 tbsp whole caraway seeds

1 tbsp vegetable oil

1 red onion, halved and thinly sliced

2 tbsp brown sugar

1 small red cabbage, shredded

2 apples, peeled and thinly sliced

2 tbsp red wine

125 ml/4 fl oz apple juice

2 tbsp **caraway and cider vinegar**

salt and freshly ground black pepper

1 tsp lemon juice

Serves 6

Red cabbage absorbs new flavours extremely well, and the addition of the vinegar makes this a delicious side dish.

In a saucepan over a medium heat, dry roast the caraway seeds for about 1 minute until they start to give off an aroma.

Heat the oil in a large saucepan over a medium heat, add the onion and sauté for 5 minutes until it becomes translucent. Add the brown sugar, stir, then add the cabbage and apples. Stir for a few minutes until the cabbage wilts. Pour in the red wine, apple juice and vinegar. Add the toasted caraway seeds, and salt and pepper to taste. Bring the mixture to the boil, lower to a simmer, add the lemon juice, cover and cook for 30 minutes.

Note: braised cabbage is wonderful served with chicken or meat dishes.

Mango, Pepper and Pineapple Salsa

1 tbsp olive oil

1 tsp brown sugar

1 mango, peeled and diced

115 g/4 oz pineapple chunks

$1/2$ red pepper, diced

$1/2$ yellow pepper, diced

$1/2$ green pepper, diced

2 tbsp **mango, tarragon and champagne vinegar**

salt and freshly ground black pepper

5 g/ $1/8$ oz tarragon leaves, chopped

Makes about 250 g/9 oz

This salsa is so colourful and tasty that you will look for dishes to serve it with: grilled swordfish, steamed bass and even barbecued chicken all complement it perfectly.

Heat the olive oil in a frying pan over a high heat. Add the brown sugar and stir.

As soon as the sugar dissolves, add the mango, pineapple and peppers. Keep stirring over a high heat and slowly pour in the vinegar. Add the salt and pepper, and the tarragon leaves, and stir for another minute or two. Keep an eye on this - you want the ingredients just to char slightly but not really cook. Remove from the heat and serve warm.

Lemon Grass, Ginger and Garlic Vinegar

This is a wonderfully exotic vinegar, inspired by South-east Asian cuisine.

2 stalks lemon grass

3 garlic cloves, peeled

1 tbsp grated ginger

250 ml/9 fl oz rice wine vinegar

Wash and dry the lower portion of the lemon grass stalks, then crush or bruise them slightly. Cut them if you would like smaller pieces in the jar. Cut the garlic cloves in half lengthways.

Place the lemon grass, garlic and ginger in a clean jar.

In a saucepan over a medium heat, heat the rice wine vinegar until it starts to bubble around the edges of the pan. Remove from the heat, cool a little, then add to the jar with the other ingredients. When completely cool, cover the jar and store in a dark, dry place.

Note: if rice wine (a staple of Asian cuisine) is not available, use cider vinegar or plain white vinegar instead.

Ginger and Star Anise Vinegar

Try this vinegar on a salad, or even better in chutney, because these three ingredients are simply delicious when combined.

250 ml/9 fl oz red wine vinegar

3 whole star anise

4-cm/1$\frac{1}{2}$-inch piece fresh ginger, sliced

Bring the red wine vinegar to the boil in a saucepan over a medium heat, then simmer for 2 minutes. Remove from the heat, add the star anise and ginger and leave to cool.

Pour the mixture into a clean jar. Cover and keep in a dark place or refrigerate. Test for taste and filter out the star anise and ginger when ready to use.

Lemon Grass, Ginger and Garlic Vinegar

Asian Coleslaw

4 tbsp **lemon grass, ginger and garlic vinegar**

2 tbsp sugar

$^1/_4$ tsp salt

125 ml/4 fl oz mayonnaise

$^1/_2$ head large green cabbage, shredded

2 carrots, grated

40 g/1$^1/_2$ oz cashew nuts, crushed

Serves 4-6

Once you have made this mouthwatering variation of traditional coleslaw, you will find it difficult to go back to the original!

To make the marinade, combine the vinegar and sugar in a small saucepan and stir over a medium heat until the sugar is dissolved. Remove from the heat and add the salt and mayonnaise.

Combine the shredded cabbage and carrots in a large bowl. Add the marinade and toss well. Transfer to a serving bowl, scatter the cashew nuts on top and serve.

Lemon Grass, Ginger and Garlic Vinegar

Skewered Prawns with Lemon Grass Yogurt Dip

Prawns

4 stalks lemon grass

24 tiger prawns

coarse salt and freshly ground pepper, to garnish

Dip

175 ml/6 fl oz natural yogurt

2 tbsp **lemon grass, ginger and garlic vinegar**

1 cucumber, peeled and diced

1 garlic clove, crushed

$1/2$ tsp salt

dash of white pepper

$1/2$ lemon, juiced

$1/2$ tsp grated fresh ginger

Serves 4

This dish is lots of fun to serve at a party - your guests will love having the prawns served on lemon grass skewers, and the dip is absolutely delicious.

To prepare the prawns, cut each lemon grass stalk in half lengthways and trim to pieces 30 cm/12 inches long. Using a sharp knife, whittle away the end of each lemon grass stalk to form a pointed end.

Peel and devein the prawns. Thread 3 prawns on to each lemon grass stalk by carefully inserting the pointed end of the stalk into one side of the thick part of the prawn and then out the other side. Bend the prawn a little and thread the stalk again into the less meaty part. Repeat the process so that each lemon grass stalk has 3 prawns that have been pierced twice.

Cook the prawns on a hot barbecue for about 2 minutes on each side - just until they turn pink.

To make the dip, combine the dip ingredients, mix well and transfer to a

serving bowl. If not using immediately, cover with clingfilm and store in the refrigerator.

Arrange the prawn skewers on a platter and sprinkle with coarse salt and freshly ground black pepper. Serve with a bowl of the lemon grass yogurt dip.

Ginger and Star Anise Vinegar

Apricot and Fig Chutney

125 ml/4 fl oz **ginger and star anise vinegar**

125 ml/4 fl oz apple cider

125 ml/4 fl oz water

1 red onion, coarsely chopped

4 tbsp brown sugar

4-cm/1^1/$_2$-inch piece fresh ginger, sliced

^{1}/$_8$ tsp black peppercorns, slightly crushed

165 g/5 ^{3}/$_4$ oz dried apricots (about 20), chopped

6 dried figs, stems removed and chopped

Makes about 175 g/6 oz

Try this recipe with dried fruit or fresh fruit – whichever you prefer. Chutneys are wonderful and they make a great accompaniment to turkey or meat dishes.

Combine the vinegar, cider and water in a saucepan over a medium-high heat. Add the onion, cook for 2 minutes, then add the brown sugar. Continue to stir over a medium heat then add the remaining ingredients. Bring to the boil, lower the heat and simmer until all the liquid is absorbed. Add more boiling water if it is used up and the fruit is still not tender. You can add 1 star anise from the vinegar, but remove it after cooking.

Adjust the seasonings to taste, leave to cool, transfer to a bowl with a lid and refrigerate.

Rosemary and Garlic Balsamic Vinegar

The combination of rosemary and garlic makes this one of the most fragrant vinegars, and it tastes every bit as good as it smells!

ten 5-cm/2-inch sprigs rosemary

4 garlic cloves

250 ml/9 fl oz balsamic vinegar

Wash the rosemary sprigs, dry and tear off the leaves from the stems. Split the garlic cloves in half lengthways. Combine the leaves and garlic halves in a clean jar.

In a saucepan over a medium heat, heat the balsamic vinegar until it just starts to bubble around the edges of the pan. Wait until it cools a little, then pour into the jar with the rosemary and garlic. When it is completely cool, cover the jar and store in a cool, dark place. Check occasionally to see whether the vinegar has reached the desired strength.

Before using, strain the vinegar through a fine sieve or muslin into clean jars. Add a fresh sprig of rosemary for decoration and again cover and store in a cool, dark place.

Basil, Chive and Lemon Vinegar

This fresh-tasting vinegar is very useful for transforming salads when you have unexpected guests.

zest of ½ lemon

5 basil leaves

10 stalks chives

250 ml/9 fl oz white wine vinegar

When peeling the lemon for the zest (using only half the lemon), be sure to avoid the white pith. Wash and dry the basil leaves and the chives, then crush them or chop roughly. Place the zest, basil and chives in a clean jar.

In a saucepan over a medium heat, heat the white wine vinegar until it starts to bubble around the edges of the pan. Wait until it cools just a little, then add it to the jar with the other ingredients. When it is completely cool, cover the jar and store in a cool, dark and dry place.

Grilled Field Mushrooms with Rosemary Garlic Drizzle

8 fresh field mushrooms

2 tbsp olive oil

salt and freshly ground black pepper

5 tbsp **rosemary and garlic balsamic vinegar**

fresh Parmesan cheese

rosemary sprigs, to garnish

Serves 2-4

There is something very special about the flavour of field mushrooms combined with balsamic vinegar. Add rosemary and garlic, and it is pure heaven!

Preheat the grill. Clean the mushrooms and remove the stems. Place the mushrooms on a baking sheet and brush both sides with olive oil. Sprinkle with salt and pepper, then grill for about 3 minutes. Turn over and grill the other side.

While the mushrooms are grilling, pour the rosemary and garlic balsamic vinegar into a saucepan and bring to the boil. Lower the heat and simmer for several minutes until the mixture starts to reduce.

When the mushrooms are soft, remove from the grill, place on a serving platter and drizzle over the reduced vinegar. Grate the Parmesan on top, decorate with a rosemary sprig and serve immediately.

Marinated Rosemary and Garlic Chicken Breasts

4 tbsp **rosemary and garlic balsamic vinegar**

125 ml/4 fl oz olive oil

4 garlic cloves, crushed

salt and freshly ground black pepper

900 g/2 lb chicken breasts, boned and skinned

rosemary sprigs, to garnish

Serves 4-6

This recipe is really simple and truly delicious. It keeps several days in the refrigerator, so make a batch and grill the chicken whenever you feel like it.

To make the marinade, combine the vinegar, oil and garlic and mix well. Season with salt and pepper to taste.

Pound the chicken breasts until thin and place in the marinade. Cover and refrigerate at least overnight.

When ready to cook, remove the breasts from the marinade and season with salt and pepper. Heat a frying pan or griddle pan over a high heat, add the chicken breasts and sauté on both sides until cooked through. Discard the remaining marinade – do not use it again since the raw chicken was marinating in it.

Serve the chicken breasts immediately, garnished with fresh rosemary sprigs.

Basil, Chive and Lemon Vinegar

Warm Potato and Artichoke Salad with Basil, Chive and Lemon Dressing

450–675 g/1–1½ lb small potatoes

5 artichoke bottoms, cooked

25 g/1 oz pickles, chopped

1 tbsp chopped fresh dill

20 stalks chives, chopped

4 tbsp **basil, chive and lemon vinegar**

1 tsp Dijon mustard

2 tbsp olive oil

1 tbsp fresh lemon juice

salt and freshly ground black pepper

Serves 4-6

This is a great summer salad – the potatoes and artichokes go beautifully with the basil, chive and lemon dressing.

Clean the potatoes, leaving the skins on, and cook in boiling water until soft. Cut into bite-sized pieces. Cut the cooked artichoke bottoms into bite-sized pieces and combine in a mixing bowl with the cooked potatoes. Add the pickles, dill and chives.

Whisk together the vinegar, mustard, olive oil and lemon juice. Season with salt and pepper to taste. Pour over the potato and artichoke mixture and mix.

Serve immediately or store covered in the refrigerator and bring to room temperature before serving.

Fig and Spice Vinegar

This vinegar is perfect for spicing up winter dishes - the distinctive aroma of the cinnamon and cloves will remind you of all things festive.

6 whole dried figs, **stems removed,** quartered

175 ml/6 fl oz cider vinegar

4 tbsp balsamic vinegar

2 tbsp sugar

$1/2$ tsp cinnamon

1 tsp ground cloves

$1/4$ tsp vanilla

Cut the figs into quarters.

Add all the ingredients to a saucepan and bring to the boil slowly over a medium heat. Simmer for 2 minutes. Remove from the heat, leave to cool, pour into a clean jar and cover. Store in a cool, dark place.

Pomegranate and Vanilla Vinegar

The combination of the pomegranate seeds and the vanilla extract makes a glorious colour. When stored in a pretty glass jar, this will look lovely on display in your kitchen.

250 ml/9 fl oz white wine vinegar

60 g/2¼ oz pomegranate seeds

1 tsp vanilla extract

Heat the white wine vinegar in a saucepan over a medium heat. Bring to the boil and simmer for 2 minutes.

Pour the pomegranate seeds and vanilla into a clean jar. When the vinegar has cooled a little, add it to the jar. Cover and filter out the seeds within 2 weeks. Store in a cool, dark place or refrigerate.

Baked Cheese and Spiced Fig Puffs

450 g/1 lb frozen puff pastry
(1 sheet)

butter, for greasing

plain flour, for dusting

1 egg, beaten

115 g/4 oz cream cheese

55 g/2 oz Roquefort

55 g/2 oz goat's cheese

140 g/1½ oz pistachio nuts, chopped

2 tbsp **fig and spice vinegar**

Serves 6

Your guests will love this appetizer. The puffs look good, taste delicious and are perfect for the start of a wonderful party.

For the pastry puffs, defrost the pastry sheet in the refrigerator (preferably overnight).

Preheat the oven to 200°C/400°F/Gas Mark 6. Grease two 12-cup muffin tins. Prepare a floured work surface and lay out the pastry sheet on top of it. Roll out to a thickness of 3 mm/⅛ inch. Cut out circles of dough slightly larger than the circumference of the holes in a muffin tin. Place each circle of dough into each muffin hole. Spread out to cover the bottom and a little way up the sides. Brush the surface with the beaten egg.

Place in the oven and bake for about 12 minutes, until the pastry puffs begin to turn golden. Remove from the oven, leave to cool and remove the pastry 'muffins' from the tins.

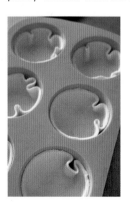

For the filling, combine the cheeses and chopped pistachio nuts in a food processor. Process until well blended. Cover and refrigerate until ready to use.

When ready to serve, take the fig quarters out of the vinegar and cut into smaller pieces. Divide the cheese mixture between six of the pastry muffins, top each with a small piece of fig and drizzle over the vinegar. Place the remaining pastry muffins on top. Put on a baking sheet and bake for 1-2 minutes until the cheese melts. Serve immediately.

Salmon Carpaccio with Pomegranate Seeds and Basil

450 g/1 lb salmon fillet, skinned and sliced paper thin

125 ml/4 fl oz olive oil

3 tbsp **pomegranate and vanilla vinegar**

2 tbsp freshly squeezed lemon juice

salt and freshly ground black pepper

5 g/$^{1}/_{8}$ oz fresh basil leaves, chopped

zest of $^{1}/_{2}$ lemon, cut into thin strips

60 g/2$^{1}/_{4}$ oz fresh pomegranate seeds

Serves 6

This is a perfect dish for a weekend brunch. It looks beautiful and takes no time at all to prepare!

Arrange the salmon slices on a serving platter large enough to accommodate all of them without overlapping.

Whisk together the olive oil, vinegar and lemon juice. Season to taste with salt and pepper and pour over the salmon slices. Cover with clingfilm and refrigerate for at least 30 minutes.

Remove the clingfilm from the serving platter and sprinkle the salmon with the basil leaves, strips of lemon zest and pomegranate seeds.

Note: this recipe calls for raw salmon, but you can easily substitute smoked salmon.

Sautéed Pears with Whipped Yogurt and Pomegranate Cassis Reduction

3 tbsp **pomegranate and vanilla vinegar**

2 tbsp crème de cassis

2 tsp maple syrup

135 ml/4 ½ fl oz double cream

freshly ground black pepper

2 pears, peeled and thinly sliced

1 tsp sugar

5 tbsp full-fat natural yogurt

fresh mint leaves, to garnish

Serves 4

This dish not only sounds sophisticated, but it tastes very extravagant – perfect for when you want to impress!

In a small frying pan over a medium-high heat, combine the vinegar, crème de cassis and maple syrup. Keep stirring over the heat as the mixture reduces and becomes syrupy. After about 4 minutes, add 1 tablespoon of cream and a dash of black pepper. Lower the heat, keep stirring, then, right before you serve it, add the sliced pears and sauté for another minute. The pears should be nicely coated, but keep an eye on them. Make sure the syrup does not burn.

In a mixing bowl, beat the remaining cream until it starts to thicken, then add the sugar and keep whipping. When peaks form, stop beating and fold in the yogurt.

Remove the pears from the pan and place on serving plates. Top with the whipped cream and yogurt mixture, drizzle a little pomegranate syrup over them and serve garnished with fresh mint leaves.

Index